A family keepsake

Celebrating Christmas for the

_____

Family

For the years

_____ *to* _____

Year: 20 ___

Our Christmas Connections

We celebrated the Christmas season with these special people:

Write the names of the family and friends that you celebrated Christmas with this year.

Our Special Christmas Places

We celebrated the Christmas season at the following places.

Describe where you were for Christmas parties, Community Events, Christmas Day, Boxing Day, New Years…

Our Christmas Story

Christmas was special this year because...

Describe Christmas in your family, special moments, foods, traditions, decorations, craft, gifts or stories.

_____
_____
_____
_____
_____
_____
_____
_____
_____
_____
_____

Our Year in Review

Special moments from this year include:

Reflect on achievements, special events, milestones reached and memories from the past year.

_____
_____
_____
_____
_____
_____
_____
_____
_____
_____
_____

Year: 20 ___

Our Christmas Connections

We celebrated the Christmas season with these special people:
Write the names of the family and friends that you celebrated Christmas with this year.

_____   _____   _____
_____   _____   _____
_____   _____   _____
_____   _____   _____
_____   _____   _____
_____   _____   _____
_____   _____   _____
_____   _____   _____
_____   _____   _____

Our Special Christmas Places

We celebrated the Christmas season at the following places.
Describe where you were for Christmas parties, Community Events, Christmas Day, Boxing Day, New Years…

_____
_____
_____
_____
_____
_____
_____
_____
_____
_____
_____

Our Christmas Story

Christmas was special this year because...
Describe Christmas in your family, special moments, foods, traditions, decorations, craft, gifts or stories.

Our Year in Review

Special moments from this year include:
Reflect on achievements, special events, milestones reached and memories from the past year.

Year: 20 ___

Our Christmas Connections

We celebrated the Christmas season with these special people:

Write the names of the family and friends that you celebrated Christmas with this year.

Our Special Christmas Places

We celebrated the Christmas season at the following places.

Describe where you were for Christmas parties, Community Events, Christmas Day, Boxing Day, New Years...

Our Christmas Story

Christmas was special this year because...
Describe Christmas in your family, special moments, foods, traditions, decorations, craft, gifts or stories.

_____
_____
_____
_____
_____
_____
_____
_____
_____
_____
_____
_____
_____

Our Year in Review

Special moments from this year include:
Reflect on achievements, special events, milestones reached and memories from the past year.

_____
_____
_____
_____
_____
_____
_____
_____
_____
_____
_____

Year: 20 ___

Our Christmas Connections

We celebrated the Christmas season with these special people:

Write the names of the family and friends that you celebrated Christmas with this year.

_____   _____   _____
_____   _____   _____
_____   _____   _____
_____   _____   _____
_____   _____   _____
_____   _____   _____
_____   _____   _____
_____   _____   _____
_____   _____   _____
_____   _____   _____

Our Special Christmas Places

We celebrated the Christmas season at the following places.

Describe where you were for Christmas parties, Community Events, Christmas Day, Boxing Day, New Years...

_____
_____
_____
_____
_____
_____
_____
_____
_____
_____
_____
_____

Our Christmas Story

Christmas was special this year because...
Describe Christmas in your family, special moments, foods, traditions, decorations, craft, gifts or stories.

_____
_____
_____
_____
_____
_____
_____
_____
_____
_____
_____
_____

Our Year in Review

Special moments from this year include:
Reflect on achievements, special events, milestones reached and memories from the past year.

_____
_____
_____
_____
_____
_____
_____
_____
_____
_____

Year: 20 ____

Our Christmas Connections

We celebrated the Christmas season with these special people:

Write the names of the family and friends that you celebrated Christmas with this year.

_____ _____ _____
_____ _____ _____
_____ _____ _____
_____ _____ _____
_____ _____ _____
_____ _____ _____
_____ _____ _____
_____ _____ _____
_____ _____ _____

Our Special Christmas Places

We celebrated the Christmas season at the following places.

Describe where you were for Christmas parties, Community Events, Christmas Day, Boxing Day, New Years…

_____
_____
_____
_____
_____
_____
_____
_____
_____
_____

Our Christmas Story

Christmas was special this year because…

Describe Christmas in your family, special moments, foods, traditions, decorations, craft, gifts or stories.

_____
_____
_____
_____
_____
_____
_____
_____
_____
_____
_____
_____

Our Year in Review

Special moments from this year include:

Reflect on achievements, special events, milestones reached and memories from the past year.

_____
_____
_____
_____
_____
_____
_____
_____
_____
_____

Year: 20 ___

Our Christmas Connections

We celebrated the Christmas season with these special people:

Write the names of the family and friends that you celebrated Christmas with this year.

_____   _____   _____
_____   _____   _____
_____   _____   _____
_____   _____   _____
_____   _____   _____
_____   _____   _____
_____   _____   _____
_____   _____   _____
_____   _____   _____
_____   _____   _____

Our Special Christmas Places

We celebrated the Christmas season at the following places.

Describe where you were for Christmas parties, Community Events, Christmas Day, Boxing Day, New Years…

_____
_____
_____
_____
_____
_____
_____
_____
_____
_____
_____

Our Christmas Story

Christmas was special this year because...
Describe Christmas in your family, special moments, foods, traditions, decorations, craft, gifts or stories.

_____
_____
_____
_____
_____
_____
_____
_____
_____
_____
_____
_____
_____

Our Year in Review

Special moments from this year include:
Reflect on achievements, special events, milestones reached and memories from the past year.

_____
_____
_____
_____
_____
_____
_____
_____
_____
_____

Year: 20 ___

Our Christmas Connections

We celebrated the Christmas season with these special people:

Write the names of the family and friends that you celebrated Christmas with this year.

_____   _____   _____
_____   _____   _____
_____   _____   _____
_____   _____   _____
_____   _____   _____
_____   _____   _____
_____   _____   _____
_____   _____   _____
_____   _____   _____

Our Special Christmas Places

We celebrated the Christmas season at the following places.

Describe where you were for Christmas parties, Community Events, Christmas Day, Boxing Day, New Years…

_____
_____
_____
_____
_____
_____
_____
_____
_____
_____
_____
_____

Our Christmas Story

Christmas was special this year because…
Describe Christmas in your family, special moments, foods, traditions, decorations, craft, gifts or stories.

_____
_____
_____
_____
_____
_____
_____
_____
_____
_____
_____
_____

Our Year in Review

Special moments from this year include:
Reflect on achievements, special events, milestones reached and memories from the past year.

_____
_____
_____
_____
_____
_____
_____
_____
_____
_____
_____
_____

Year: 20 ___

Our Christmas Connections

We celebrated the Christmas season with these special people:

Write the names of the family and friends that you celebrated Christmas with this year.

_____   _____   _____
_____   _____   _____
_____   _____   _____
_____   _____   _____
_____   _____   _____
_____   _____   _____
_____   _____   _____
_____   _____   _____
_____   _____   _____
_____   _____   _____

Our Special Christmas Places

We celebrated the Christmas season at the following places.

Describe where you were for Christmas parties, Community Events, Christmas Day, Boxing Day, New Years…

_____
_____
_____
_____
_____
_____
_____
_____
_____
_____
_____

Our Christmas Story

Christmas was special this year because…
Describe Christmas in your family, special moments, foods, traditions, decorations, craft, gifts or stories.

_____
_____
_____
_____
_____
_____
_____
_____
_____
_____
_____
_____
_____

Our Year in Review

Special moments from this year include:
Reflect on achievements, special events, milestones reached and memories from the past year.

_____
_____
_____
_____
_____
_____
_____
_____
_____
_____
_____

Year: 20 ____

Our Christmas Connections

We celebrated the Christmas season with these special people:

Write the names of the family and friends that you celebrated Christmas with this year.

_____   _____   _____
_____   _____   _____
_____   _____   _____
_____   _____   _____
_____   _____   _____
_____   _____   _____
_____   _____   _____
_____   _____   _____
_____   _____   _____

Our Special Christmas Places

We celebrated the Christmas season at the following places.

Describe where you were for Christmas parties, Community Events, Christmas Day, Boxing Day, New Years...

_____
_____
_____
_____
_____
_____
_____
_____
_____
_____
_____

Our Christmas Story

Christmas was special this year because…

Describe Christmas in your family, special moments, foods, traditions, decorations, craft, gifts or stories.

_____
_____
_____
_____
_____
_____
_____
_____
_____
_____
_____
_____

Our Year in Review

Special moments from this year include:

Reflect on achievements, special events, milestones reached and memories from the past year.

_____
_____
_____
_____
_____
_____
_____
_____
_____
_____
_____

Year: 20 ___

Our Christmas Connections

We celebrated the Christmas season with these special people:

Write the names of the family and friends that you celebrated Christmas with this year.

_____   _____   _____
_____   _____   _____
_____   _____   _____
_____   _____   _____
_____   _____   _____
_____   _____   _____
_____   _____   _____
_____   _____   _____
_____   _____   _____
_____   _____   _____

Our Special Christmas Places

We celebrated the Christmas season at the following places.

Describe where you were for Christmas parties, Community Events, Christmas Day, Boxing Day, New Years...

_____
_____
_____
_____
_____
_____
_____
_____
_____
_____
_____

Our Christmas Story

Christmas was special this year because…
Describe Christmas in your family, special moments, foods, traditions, decorations, craft, gifts or stories.

_____
_____
_____
_____
_____
_____
_____
_____
_____
_____
_____
_____

Our Year in Review

Special moments from this year include:
Reflect on achievements, special events, milestones reached and memories from the past year.

_____
_____
_____
_____
_____
_____
_____
_____
_____
_____
_____

www.ingramcontent.com/pod-product-compliance
Lightning Source LLC
Chambersburg PA
CBHW041430010526
44107CB00046B/1566